15 Full Days of Faith for prosperity is ……….

Contents

15 Full Days of Faith for prosperity is 1

Copyright 4

Disclaimer: 5

Faith is a mother uttering this prayer and believing it into its highest form. 6

Day 2: 7

Faith is a son uttering this prayer and believing it into its highest form. 7

Day 3: 8

Faith is a disable person uttering this prayer and believing it into its highest form. 8

Day 4 : 9

Faith is a pastor uttering this prayer and believing it into its highest form. 9

…Continued prayer from Day 4: 10

Day 5 : 11

Faith is a grandmother uttering this prayer and believing it into its highest form. 11

…Continued prayer from Day 5: 12

Day 6 : 13

Faith is a grandfather uttering this prayer and believing it into its highest form. 13

Day 7: 14

Faith is a young woman getting married for the first time uttering this prayer and believing it into its highest form. 14

Day 8 : 15

Faith is a business woman uttering this prayer and believing it into its highest form. 15

Day 9: 16

Faith is a business man uttering this prayer and believing it into its highest form. 16

Day 10: 17

Faith is a General Manager uttering this prayer and believing it into its highest form. 17

Day 11 : 18

Faith is a Custodian uttering this prayer and believing it into its highest form. 18

Day 12: 20

Faith is an editor uttering this prayer and believing it into its highest form. 20

Day 13: 21

Faith is an unemployed person uttering this prayer and believing it into its highest form. 21

Day 14: 22

Faith is a faithful tithing being given to god while uttering this prayer and believing it into its highest form. 22

Day 15: 23

Faith is a mother of a sick child uttering this prayer and believing it into its highest form. 23

Make sure to make regular contributions to your church 24

Right a Vision and Make it plain -Thoughts and Notes 25

Right a Vision and Make it plain -Thoughts and Notes 26

Right a Vision and Make it plain -Thoughts and Notes 27

References 28

Copyright © 2014 by Pen Name AB

All rights reserved. This book or any portion thereof may not be reproduced or used in any manner whatsoever without the written permission of the publisher and/or author except for the use of brief quotations in a book review.

ISBN-13: 978-0985952730

(Pen Name AB) –Author will remain anonymous

ISBN-10: 0985952733

Printed in the United States of America

For permission requests and ordering information, write to the publisher:

Attention: Book Coordinator

HCITSC, LLC

1911 SW Campus Drive Ste 555

Federal Way, Washington 98023

Disclaimer:

This book and the content in the book doesn't provide any guarantee of any kind. When reading this book please take in consideration that the authors and or readers opinions in regards to the definition of prosperity can vary .

Day 1:

Faith is a mother uttering this prayer and believing it into its highest form.

Lord hear my complete prayer,

Oh lord give me the great strength that comes from faith in you God. Lord protect and heal me and my children from all sickness , addictions , and afflictions .

Lord give me and my children a covering that includes all godly benefits towards us.

Oh lord provide me , and my children with a protective covering filled with prosperity, filled with an understanding of how to be drug free , filled with an understanding of how to be disease free , and Oh lord give us all the wisdom and knowledge needed to complete our task safely .

Remind me lord that the lord is my shepherd I shall not want (r2 pg1). . Lord I surrender all my and my family's financial concerns to you .Lord I completely trust and pray that all my finances and all my debts will be paid without stress and without harm to me and without harm to my family .

Lord I trust and pray that you lord will give me and my family constant stress free financial stability, without any harm to me and without harm to my family .

Lord I complete my prayer .The lord is my Shepard I shall not want (r2 pg1).

Day 2:

Faith is a son uttering this prayer and believing it into its highest form.

Lord hear my complete prayer,

Guide me lord with your protection and wisdom. Oh lord forgive me of my sins.

Lord watch over me lord during the daytime and the night. Lord please heal any negative emotions in my heart.

Lord protect my mother and father and help them protect me. Lord I pray for the guidance of your holy spirit.

Help me lord to make the right decisions and help me to know when to walk away. Protect me lord

Remind me lord that the lord is my shepherd I shall not want (r2 pg1). Lord I surrender all my and my family's financial concerns to you .Lord I completely trust and pray that all my finances and all my debts will be paid without stress and without harm to me and without harm to my family .

Lord I trust and pray that you lord will give me and my family constant stress free financial stability, without any harm to me and without harm to my family .

Lord I complete my prayer .The lord is my Shepard I shall not want (r2 pg1).

Day 3:

Faith is a disable person uttering this prayer and believing it into its highest form.

Lord hear my complete prayer, Oh lord renew my mind, body and soul lord. Lord I come before you today in need of your healing of all things .

Oh lord give me the daily strength and guidance to move forward on the path that you've made just for me. Lord guide me towards better health.

Lord guide me towards wisdom to identify those you've placed around me to help. Oh Lord I praise and thank you for all that you've given me.

Oh lord continue to give me strength. Lord watch over me lord during the daytime and the night. Lord please heal any negative emotions in my heart.

Remind me lord that the lord is my shepherd I shall not want (r2 pg1). Lord I surrender all my and my family's financial concerns to you .Lord I completely trust and pray that all my finances and all my debts will be paid without stress and without harm to me and without harm to my family .

Lord I trust and pray that you lord will give me and my family constant stress free financial stability, without any harm to me and without harm to my family .

Lord I complete my prayer .The lord is my Shepard I shall not want (r2 pg. 1).

Day 4 :

Faith is a pastor uttering this prayer and believing it into its highest form.

Lord hear my complete prayer ,

Guide me , my wife and my congregation lord with your protection and wisdom. Oh lord forgive me , my wife and my congregation of our sins.

Lord Watch over me , my wife and my congregation lord during the daytime and the night . Lord please heal any negative emotions in our heart .

Send the sword lord of your holy spirit to sever and break all spells, curses ,hexes , and remove all other negative genetic situations , remove harmful negative intergenerational situations , remove negative and harmful addictive situations that are past present or to come and that are known and unknown against me , my relationships , my congregation , my family , my finances , possessions ,all individuals that I mentor, and my ministry as a whole .

Through the name , power , blood , of Jesus Christ , Lord I need you to sever and break the power and the affect in and around me , my wife and my congregation of any evil spirits and their companions sprits .

Oh lord provide me , and my children, and my congregation with a protective covering filled with prosperity, filled with an understanding of how to be drug free , filled with an understanding of how to be disease free , and Oh lord give us all the wisdom and knowledge needed to complete our task safely .

…Continued prayer from Day 4:

Remind me lord that the lord is my shepherd I shall not want (r2 pg1). . Lord I surrender all my , my wife , my children , my congregations, and my family's financial concerns to you.

Lord I completely trust and pray that all my finances and all my debts will be paid without stress and without harm to me and without harm to my family .

Lord I trust and pray that you lord will give me and my family constant stress free financial stability, without any harm to me and without harm to my family .

Lord I complete my prayer .The lord is my Shepard I shall not want (r2 pg1).

Day 5 :

Faith is a grandmother uttering this prayer and believing it into its highest form.

Lord hear my complete prayer,

Heavenly father I praise and thank you for all have given to me. Please cover me with the protective precious blood of your son Jesus Christ and increase your holy spirit in me with your gifts of wisdom, knowledge, and understanding, and hunger for to be in your blessings for eternity .

Father please heal my negative emotions and any wounds in my heart and spirit.

Send the sword lord of your holy spirit to sever and break all spells, curses ,hexes , and remove all other negative genetic situations , remove harmful negative intergenerational situations , remove negative and harmful addictive situations that are past present or to come and that are known and unknown against me , my relationships, my family , my finances , possessions.

Through the name , power , blood , of Jesus Christ , Lord I need you to sever and break the power and the affect in and around me ,my children and my family of any evil spirits and their companions sprits .

Oh lord provide me , and my children with a protective covering filled with prosperity, filled with an understanding of how to be drug free , filled with an understanding of how to be disease free , and Oh lord give us all the wisdom and knowledge needed to complete our task safely .

…Continued prayer from Day 5:

Remind me lord that the lord is my shepherd I shall not want (r2 pg1). Lord I surrender all my and my family's financial concerns to you .Lord I completely trust and pray that all my finances and all my debts will be paid without stress and without harm to me and without harm to my family .

Lord I trust and pray that you lord will give me and my family constant stress free financial stability, without any harm to me and without harm to my family.

Lord I complete my prayer .The lord is my Shepard I shall not want (r2 pg1).

Day 6 :

Faith is a grandfather uttering this prayer and believing it into its highest form.

Lord hear my complete prayer ,

Lord I ask that you please a hedge of protection around me and my family that hides us from the enemy and hides us from all demon spirits . Lord make it impossible for the enemy to track or trace me and lord make it impossible for all demon spirits to track and trace me .

Lord keep me and my children from free from evil , free from ungodly temptation , free from drugs, free from Satan's attacks and free from afflictions.

Remind me lord that the lord is my shepherd I shall not want (R2 pg1). Lord I surrender all my and my family's financial concerns to you .Lord I completely trust and pray that all my finances and all my debts will be paid without stress and without harm to me and without harm to my family .

Lord I trust and pray that you lord will give me and my family constant stress free financial stability, without any harm to me and without harm to my family.

Lord I complete my prayer .The lord is my Shepard I shall not want (R2 pg1).

Day 7:

Faith is a young woman getting married for the first time uttering this prayer and believing it into its highest form.

Lord hear my complete prayer ,

Lord I come before you today in need of your healing . Lord in you all things are possible . Lord Hold my heart within yours and lord renew my mind , renew my body , and renew my soul . Lord give me the strength to move forward on the path you've laid out for me . Lord guide me towards better health and lord give me the wisdom .

Lord give me the wisdom to identify those you've placed around me to help me.

Lord I pray over my mind .Lord help me to defeat the lies , lord help me to defeat the thoughts of insecurity and lord help me to defeat fear , lord help me to defeat my enemy . I pray that lord you renew my mind and set my eyes on you .

Remind me lord that the lord is my shepherd I shall not want (r2 pg1). Lord I surrender all my and my family's financial concerns to you .Lord I completely trust and pray that all my finances and all my debts will be paid without stress and without harm to me and without harm to my family .

Lord I trust and pray that you lord will give me and my family constant stress free financial stability, without any harm to me and without harm to my family .

Lord I complete my prayer .The lord is my Shepard I shall not want (r2 pg1).

Day 8 :

Faith is a business woman uttering this prayer and believing it into its highest form.

Lord hear my complete prayer ,

Lord I come before you today in need of your healing . Lord in you all things are possible . Lord Hold my heart within yours and lord renew my mind , renew my body , and renew my soul . Lord give me the strength to move forward on the path you've laid out for me . Lord guide me towards better health and lord give me the wisdom .

Lord give me the wisdom to identify those you've placed around me to help me get stronger and more successful in my works .

Lord I pray over my mind .Lord help me to defeat the lies , lord help me to defeat the thoughts of insecurity and lord help me to defeat fear , lord help me to defeat my enemy. I pray that lord you renew my mind and set my eyes on you .

Remind me lord that the lord is my shepherd I shall not want (R2 pg1). Lord I surrender all my and my family's financial concerns to you .Lord I completely trust and pray that all my finances and all my debts will be paid without stress and without harm to me and without harm to my family .

Lord I trust and pray that you lord will give me and my family constant stress free financial stability, without any harm to me and without harm to my family.

Lord I complete my prayer .The lord is my Shepard I shall not want (R2 pg1).

Day 9:

Faith is a business man uttering this prayer and believing it into its highest form.

Lord hear my complete prayer ,

Lord I come before you today in need of your healing . Lord in you all things are possible . Lord Hold my heart within yours and lord renew my mind , renew my body , and renew my soul . Lord give me the strength to move forward on the path you've laid out for me . Lord guide me towards better health and lord give me the wisdom .

Lord give me the wisdom to identify those you've placed around me to help me . Lord give me the wisdom to identify those you've placed around me to guide me . Lord give me the wisdom to identify those you've placed around me to make me a success.

Remind me lord that the lord is my shepherd I shall not want (R2 pg1). Lord I surrender all my and my family's financial concerns to you .Lord I completely trust and pray that all my finances and all my debts will be paid without stress and without harm to me and without harm to my family .

Lord I trust and pray that you lord will give me and my family constant stress free financial stability, without any harm to me and without harm to my family.

Lord I complete my prayer .The lord is my Shepard I shall not want (R2 pg1).

Day 10:

Faith is a General Manager uttering this prayer and believing it into its highest form.

Lord hear my complete prayer ,

Lord I come before you today in need of your healing . Lord in you all things are possible . Lord Hold my heart within yours and lord renew my mind , renew my body , and renew my soul . Lord give me the strength to move forward on the path you've laid out for me . Lord guide me towards better health and lord give me the wisdom .

Lord give me the wisdom to identify those you've placed around me to help me get better .

Remind me lord that the lord is my shepherd I shall not want (r2 pg1). Lord I surrender all my and my family's financial concerns to you .Lord I completely trust and pray that all my finances and all my debts will be paid without stress and without harm to me and without harm to my family .

Lord I trust and pray that you lord will give me and my family constant stress free financial stability, without any harm to me and without harm to my family.

Lord I complete my prayer .The lord is my Shepard I shall not want (r2 pg1).

Day 11 :

Faith is a Custodian uttering this prayer and believing it into its highest form.

Lord hear my complete prayer ,

Heavenly father I praise and thank you for all have given to me . Please cover me with the protective blood of your son Jesus Christ and increase your holy spirit in me with your gifts of wisdom, knowledge , and understanding , hunger for prayer.

Father please heal my negative emotions and any wounds in my heart and spirit .

Send the sword lord of your holy spirit to sever and break all spells, curses ,hexes , and remove all other negative genetic situations , remove harmful negative intergenerational situations , remove negative and harmful addictive situations that are past present or to come and that are known and unknown against me , my relationships , my family , my finances , possessions ,all individuals that I mentor, and my ministry as a whole . Oh Lord give me the great strength that comes from faith in you God.

Lord protect and heal me and my children from all sickness , addictions, and affliction.

Lord give me children and covering that includes all godly benefits towards us.

Remind me lord that the lord is my shepherd I shall not want (r2 pg1). Lord I surrender all my and my family's financial

…Continued prayer from Day 11:

concerns to you .Lord I completely trust and pray that all my finances and all my debts will be paid without stress and without harm to me and without harm to my family .

Lord I complete my prayer .The lord is my Shepard I shall not want (r2 pg1).

Day 12:

Faith is an editor uttering this prayer and believing it into its highest form.

Lord hear my complete prayer ,

Heavenly father I praise and thank you for all have given to me . Please cover me with the protective and precious blood of your son Jesus Christ and increase your holy spirit in me with your gifts of wisdom , knowledge , and understanding , hunger for pray.

Father please heal my negative emotions and any wounds in my heart and spirit .

Send the sword lord of your holy spirit to sever and break all spells ,curses ,hexes , and remove all other negative genetic situations, remove harmful negative intergenerational situations , remove negative and harmful addictive situations that are past present or to come and that are known and unknown against me , my relationships, my family , my finances , possessions ,all individuals that I mentor, and my ministry as a whole .

Remind me lord that the lord is my shepherd I shall not want (r2 pg. 1). Lord I surrender all my and my family's financial concerns to you .Lord I completely trust and pray that all my finances and all my debts will be paid without stress and without harm to me and without harm to my family . **Lord I complete my prayer .The lord is my Shepard I shall not want (r2 pg1).**

Day 13:

Faith is an unemployed person uttering this prayer and believing it into its highest form.

Lord hear my complete prayer,

Oh lord give me the great strength that comes from faith in you God.

Oh lord provide me , and my children with a protective covering filled with prosperity, filled with an understanding of how to be drug free , filled with an understanding of how to be disease free , and Oh lord give us all the wisdom and knowledge needed to complete our task safely .

Remind me lord that the lord is my shepherd I shall not want (r2 pg1). Lord I surrender all my and my family's financial concerns to you .Lord I completely trust and pray that all my finances and all my debts will be paid without stress and without harm to me and without harm to my family .

Lord I complete my prayer .The lord is my Shepard I shall not want (r2 pg1).

Day 14:

Faith is a faithful tithing being given to god while uttering this prayer and believing it into its highest form.
Lord hear my complete prayer,

Oh lord provide me , and my children with a protective covering filled with prosperity, filled with an understanding of how to be drug free , filled with an understanding of how to be disease free , and Oh lord give us all the wisdom and knowledge needed to complete our task safely .

Remind me lord that the lord is my shepherd I shall not want (r2 pg1). Lord I surrender all my and my family's financial concerns to you .Lord I completely trust and pray that all my finances and all my debts will be paid without stress and without harm to me and without harm to my family .

Lord I complete my prayer .The lord is my Shepard I shall not want (r2 pg1).

Day 15:

Faith is a mother of a sick child uttering this prayer and believing it into its highest form.

Lord hear my complete prayer,

Oh lord give me the great strength that comes from faith in you God.

Lord protect and heal me and my children from all sickness , addictions , and afflictions .

Lord give me and my children a covering that includes all godly benefits towards us.

Oh lord provide me , and my children with a protective covering filled with prosperity, filled with an understanding of how to be drug free , filled with an understanding of how to be disease free , and Oh lord give us all the wisdom and knowledge needed to complete our task safely .

Remind me lord that the lord is my shepherd I shall not want (r2 pg1). Lord I surrender all my and my family's financial concerns to you .Lord I completely trust and pray that all my finances and all my debts will be paid without stress and without harm to me and without harm to my family .

Lord I complete my prayer .The lord is my Shepard I shall not want (r2 pg1).

Final thoughts and Conclusion

Make sure to make regular contributions to your church. An important part of obedience to God is in the Law of Tithing. The law of tithing states to pay tithes faithfully. The law reads that all blessings are predicated— And when a blessing from God is obtained, it is by obedience. (r3 pg1).

" Meaning we receive blessings by obeying God's laws and when we obey God's laws there are blessings that go with it. Remember, blessings can be spiritual, temporal or both but are not always given in the way we expect(r3 pg1)..

Right a Vision and Make it plain -Thoughts and Notes

Right a Vision and Make it plain -Thoughts and Notes

Right a Vision and Make it plain -Thoughts and Notes

References

1. Prayers for special help, http://www.prayers-for-special-help.com/Prayers-for-Healing.html, retrieve on February 5, 2014,
2. Biblegateway,http://www.biblegateway.com/passage/?search=Psalm+23&version=KJV, retrieve on February 5, 2014,
3. Basics gospel principles, http://lds.about.com/od/basicsgospelprinciples/a/law_of_tithing.htm, , retrieve on February 5, 2014,

www.ingramcontent.com/pod-product-compliance
Lightning Source LLC
Chambersburg PA
CBHW070342240426
43665CB00046B/2547